These poems overwhelm us with disturbing and difficult truths. Meghna whisks beautiful lines out of her indelible experiences. The effervescence lingers long after.

Sivakami Velliangiri

Meghna seeks understanding, a safe space, in verse that is steeped in pain and deep emotion. In her journey to a place of healing, she offers us succour and kinship.

Srividya Sivakumar

Meghna explores known spaces with newness — be it the gentleness to 'learn to stitch like a delicate flower' or be it escapism by being 'shot by a shooting star'. Her poetry asks uncomfortable questions and confronts dark realities.

Madhu Raghavendra

trigger warning

poems of love and resistance

Meghna Prakash

HAWAKAL

CALCUTTA | NEW DELHI

CALCUTTA | NEW DELHI

Hawakal Publishers

33/1/2 K B Sarani, Mall Road, Calcutta 80
70-B/9 Amritpuri, East of Kailash, New Delhi 65

Email info@hawakal.com
Website www.hawakal.com

First edition August, 2020

Cover art: Priyanka Paul
Cover design: Bitan Chakraborty

ISBN: 978-81-946651-4-4

Price: 350 INR | USD 12.99

for
my grandmother
who read poetry to me as a child

ON LOVE

On Resistance

I said to the sun, "Tell me about the big bang."
The sun said, "It hurts to become."

Andrea Gibson

...my country is made
in my people's image
if they come for you, they
come for me too...

Fatimah Asghar
(If They Should Come for Us)

I am the woman who is willing to display her scars and
put them within exhibition frames. I am the madwoman
of moon days. I am the breast-beating woman who howls.
I am the woman who wills the skies to weep in my place.

Meena Kandasamy
(When I Hit You: Or,
A Portrait of the Writer as a Young Wife)

ON LOVE

LIGHT

A blunt yellow
bruise on my skin, I
showed colours
in black and white polaroid.

Your laughter
a soft pellet of rain
falling on
the roar of the waves

crashing against
my shore, the sand
creeping into
my toenails.

How hard it tries
to love me and leave me.

A LOVE MEDLEY

The plants are wilting
in a fresh cup of water

Sometimes, they die
when you care too much,

pouring more love
than asked for.

Is it why we died
when we were to bloom?

SEPARATION OF CITIES

It is quiet here, and my ears ache for the soft embrace of
your voice. Somedays, I imagine making love to the wide
spectrum of the textures with which you speak, to which
I dream about you, whispering my name.

Do your lips long for something more than the air
of the cities that have separated us? I cannot go
anywhere without you, my footsteps sink in with
heavy breaths leaving my body as I spend days
(years) without you.

Without the silver anklets adorning your
bare feet, letting me know of our summer
where someday, we will find ourselves together.

I wake up every morning
tearing, tenderly
into you.

I Learned How to Stitch Like a Delicate Flower

Your fingers tear through a silence,
A softness, a whisper that grows out my
despair.

Embrace me like flowers clasp
the summer and spring that treads on our
cheeks.

I'll quietly hide under your feet, let this darkness
gently tremble within my unkempt
shrub.

Only home to your mouth.
For me, it is enough

that you sleep
that you laugh

holding all mirth
all the pain
within the trembling
of your brave palms.

when the world in me collapses
like time.

TO FADED MEMORIES THAT HAUNT ME

These sights and smells I avoided,
but you
stayed there like a dream.

The effervescence of your existence
that rose and fell like the waves
of an ocean

echoing your name
drowning me in your depths
where the warmth shall

allow me thus
to fall asleep.
To watch the soft unfolding of rain

into the emptiness
where you reside
in a gentle love

I found a dream that I live
in the cup of quiet days
of the nonchalance

in the falling rains
where we are enough
to bear the burden of our sorrows.

With the silence
in a space that craves
your laughter

I carry it with me every day,
for I am yours
in this eternal spring

of our melancholy.
I am longing for you,
like bees hovering around petals

like a penguin meandering
past icelands for the mate
she aches.

I am holding on
to my surreal self
for you to hold me,

*calm my waves and finally
bring me home.*

WINTER LONGING

there are days / like there will be / with me yearning /
for this ache to disappear /
growing like roses on the softness of my bosom /
wrapped in the warmth /
hiding in the very folds of your chest /
where i placed my absence / with you /
for the oak tree leaves an echo / of your words /
of which I can make little sense /
but it is enough

the earth
knows my pain
living out
the daily thud
of your absence

so it carries all that you leave in it to me.

I DIED

    the July night
       you whisked away
          to quieten your life
             there are crumbled
                trails of verses
                that resonate like
                bells weeping in
                  the silence of archaic pillars
                    we build this home
                    of walls that quietly enclose
                as it shouldn't
          this longing
        you hold for me
      and my battle within the
tremors of my chest

          I am incapable of inhabiting the arms of another

Question: I am your cryptograph that you decipher
But what would you do to me when I'm naked,
and you've solved me?

Answer: In tenderness and not in longing, does it thrive—
the love that has spread like blossoms in dreams.
And in tenderness, I shall keep you when I have
solved and ravaged through counting every sweat-bead
that would form pearls on your forehead with a
sweetness of mornings.

SOME PEOPLE CAN HANDLE YOU

Some people can handle you.
Some can't. That's our truth.

I started off as a wild flower
on a cold winter night

and you,

my shivering breeze, could take me
anywhere you wanted.

So, you took me

under an elephant's foot
and a child found me afterwards

and pressed me shut in a notebook.

Men Shouldn't Rule my Heart but at 16 They Did

Master, master,
let me press your feet again.
I will kiss your very toes
if it stops you from leaving.

Master, I am lonely again.
And I will follow you
inside the wonderland
of the sheets where

I lose
sight of myself
to the intimacies
of our bodies.

Quiet Rosebuds

It's far from a memory; the sweet relish of your cherry lips
that sought an opening
like a river searching for the ocean, through cracks that
carried you into my depths.

In the spring of our longing, we unwrapped ourselves
and I found the blossom
of quiet rosebuds, drenched in the dew of desire that
evaporated into thin air

carrying our echo far into the cave of nothingness.
Carry me away from your absence into that cave
where I'd rediscover your fingers
and the sound of

laughter
that *remains*.

I Can't Forget

<table>
<tr><td>

my first kiss
it was prom night, I
had on a white dress, turned
wine into blood, my first period
I'm dancing to Clapton
you look wonderful tonight
I wore mascara, you cupped
my face, your hands
brown Girl became a moon.

your mouth telling me
I'm beautiful, I looked
at myself, your eyes
made me softer,
scars, crescent-like
naked bodies.
Commas, in the
full stops

</td><td>

I slept
in a wild
forest with
someone who
looked like
you used
to once upon a
Time.

I
mistook a
poem for
a fairytale
but I
never forgot
You.

</td></tr>
</table>

DEPARTURE

This poem is a black-silted treasury. It quietly safe-keeps all of the kindest words, your utterances of love that confounded, yet never confined you. Your rampant declarations of everything important to you – I.

Your laughter ricochets in the hollows, this damp being that remains withered in the bones of my fragile body. I can hear it almost, the tinkling sound of exuberance. The mellowness of salt sprinkled on the sea. The heartbreak of your footsteps leaving me.

Do you not see me crumbling before your eyes?

THE PAIN THE PAIN THE PAIN

crossing the opaque barriers of objects steering into the
ocean bed
of our grief, pulling the surface like a blanket smothering
the loneliness
in our existence

the pain of elbows striking against unprecedented corners,
the pain of
a thousand matches left unburnt, the pain of love devoid
of love, our feet
sink in the shadow of torn cardboard cartons that we hid in
as children

the pain of an empty playground

the pain
the pain
the pain

sounds of all the anger, the love of a single rose that has
been passed down to lovers with every thorn, every
poison, purple, purple, deep, deep dreams with slips of

paper hidden under desks, carrying snippets of future,
the antithesis of fortune cookies with gray walls against
which I break the theory of all neurons; scattered in my
skull

I exist
sans the biology of man and woman or the plateau of
culture, my feet drag to no city, transcending mad dogs
that bark quietly, as I happen to touch the unwinding of
gears in clocks, the feeling of unfeeling in emotion.

so that when you ravage me
you leave a sound

LINE OF SIGHT

I shall look up
and find you

leave behind
all that has been

for I love you
to this very day

all which is the same
all that has changed

all that is you
for you are to me

even in the hardest of days
the most beautiful

THINK OF THE COLD CORPSE LEFT IN THE ROOM

I keep looking at the leaves as if they'll kiss me, they bleed red in my dreams. When you leave, a deep, soft scar and from the chasm rises this melancholy that has been borne with sadness you've kept in hiding, in the left corner of your right eye.

I cannot ask for forgiveness for letting my body tear itself apart in your love. But I can wait till the shadow of my flesh contracts to my bones, cutting me precisely into three pieces for three nights, for three, countless days for you to see.

Love
that has crawled its way
to the earth

which now balances itself
until I read the letters
written by autumn.

For you
from me
in envelopes made from paper

that holds poems
I shall write
in the space that is still left in me.

Sadness creeps into my skin.
I'm a petal with no fragrance
and yet, you pick me off the concrete road

and tie me up in your hair.
I am as lifeless as a child
drowned, floating on shallow waters.

Will you dive before I come
clawing at you to save myself?

But instead, you kiss my trembling lips
and blow life into my mouth

memory by memory.

SILHOUETTE

there lies nothing
in a world
that goes around in circles
that bring me
to utter frailty
than your skin
that envelopes all of the universe
in warmth
leaving me

it is your fault
for turning me
into a silhouette

I Thought We'd be Magic

but as it turns out,
　　　　it was just you

being a magician
　　　　you vanish without a trace

my heart has grown wildflowers and moss
　　　　you sit across the room

searching for something.
　　　　what do you see

beyond the white walls
　　　　that imprison you?

and we've grown
　　　　in our own ways

held together by things
　　　　we could never say
to each other.

SOMEDAYS

I shiver with the loneliness
that you hold within you.

You've stayed strong
fighting it out

days and night
all seasons.

When was the last time
you smiled for yourself?

It's true,
I've always tried to understand you.

I have always loved you
but there have been days

when the walls are too high
when my feet have felt tired

of chasing you
of fighting your past

that I lie against the very wall
quietly

to make you remember
your present.

Where I stand
in a lot of ways waiting for you
to look beyond the horizon
with the scent of your hair
pushing me off a cliff.

Soft Summer Rain

Like soft summer rain

you settle into me
camping high, in the dark grey clouds.

Far away and yet your pieces
are like puzzle fragments

like tears pulled down my gravity.
And you call out to me

sharper than birds whistle to trees
and rainbows disperse within the skies

that I bow low
paying heed

to our silent conversation.
Miles away

where my sun sets
and yours rises

warming your day.
It's going to be always like this.

This distance doesn't seem
that it would be burst soon.

There's emptiness
between my lips
and loneliness in my heart.
There's no bridge between us.

And even though
eternity is a long enough wait
you leave me short interludes
of your existence

on my cheeks
a trail to my lips
and maybe,
just this one time,

I'll bring a comet back for you.

AN AFTERMATH

Perhaps lately I have been tending to my wounds.
I have come back again
for you to spit me out at your will.
For love isn't a certainty,
it's a gamble and it seems that way,
even though I am tired and lost.

I am willing to stay
perhaps not the way you want but on my
terms for the love I believe in
for the eternity that I can endure.

But know this, in all the eloquent verses,
you rise in me like
a tidal wave and wash every speck of chaos inside me,
so don't blame me for my verses,
blame your eyes that burn with flames
and turn every mortal to ash, blame your lips that melt
the coldest of hearts, even mine.
Blame your soul
for you inhabit all seasons in me.

For every time I look outside my window
from the prison of my loneliness,
you linger in me like morning dew...

An aftermath–

a quiet
soft
home.

SUNRISE

I must admit that I am too afraid to wake up.

In my dreams, I chase after wheat fields and scorpions in a sky that breaks dawn for me. Leaves lose their colour, every second that my heart realizes that only for another moment will your arms be entwined in mine. To the waking of another desolate unfulfilling day our fingers clasped in each other we wake up to some other day, unaware if only for a few moments of all that engulfs you also engulfs me.

Waking up
to distant birdcalls
and an empty bed.

the evening dust
settles like stardust
bombed cities

all the little stars
within me born of dust
this universe

Everything that I am

Everything that I am
is falling away

like a sandstorm
lost in the rages of an unhinged breeze

I am losing my mind
sifting through memories

precariously,
like a writer scrubbing those staining words

that unflatter her thoughts
and fail to conceal

the madness of her mind...

I am a cloud.
Then I am a sock
and you are nothing, nowhere.

I'm a woman
losing settlements
to torrential rains.

GROWING TENDERNESS

Grab the collar of my soul
as if I am the only one
with a heart that rages in your love
and I will revel in you
drink all of your broken bones
for there is nothing
that I want more than you.

Your laughter echoing through
the halls of our room
even when the autumn leaves turn into ashes
and scattered into the air that surrounds our lives,
Surrender to my gentle heart

that has loved through days and nights alike.

BONES AND SHADOWS

When there is a storm we always fall
but haven't we learned to sail through them too?

I am raw, made of skin and bones
I have no wings or miracles inside me.

Know that I am human
so, hold on to my fingers.

As long as you hold me
I'll hold on to you.

You, me. We are
the bits of bones, the ruins of our smashed ship

in the ocean.
I'll swim holding your ruins.

If you'll hold mine
we will keep us afloat.

Don't leave me bare to the hardships
of loneliness

with your eyes fluttering
like the wings of a butterfly.

On flames
I see your toes tracing the outline

of your shadows that have
leached out of your skin.

As the sound of your movements
found the quiet stream of existence

flowing into the ocean
that belonged to you

and the music that grappled your feet.

COAL/JEWEL

I've cracked bones / Bitten flesh / Left marks on your chest.
Remember me, will you?

I'm not a shadow you can hide / I'm fire. / I destroy, I consume, I devour.
Don't hide me in your bitter world.

I'm not a jewel / I'm coal.
I ignite your soul.

You can't break me apart / I didn't leave darling.
You ran because I burnt you.

I will lick your ashes
feast on your festering flesh,
for your bones are nothing,
but trembling memories
of my touch, and my verses.

THE CLIFF

The echo of your bones
rattled my skin
as I was singing
and writing an ode to your fingernails
that would scour through my skin

and find my soul
hiding behind the tenderness.

Of the drowsy, drunk morning
for the radio wasn't in the mood

and I wished to listen to that one song
again and again and again

till my sheep jumped off the cliff
killing themselves.

DREAM LITTLE GIRL, DREAM

There is so much sadness
that floats like a boat
towards my shore.

Where has the little girl gone?
Will she dream of making birds
out of coloured paper once again?

Will her thighs always tremble
to her cousin's touch?
She was four when she understood

that a man's touch can linger
between her breasts
long after he's gone.

THERE IS THE ESSENCE OF FREEDOM UNDER THE SOLE OF YOUR FEET

The shadows scatter onto the sand
snatched by the waves receding back to the sea
every moment passing by,
every raindrop cooped up in the clouds
pushes me back into the ghettos of nonexistence,

but I have you.

Your rose, like a voice, blossoms
under a tree that hangs
dry dreams from its naked branches,
and I know where I am going
to a place called home,

fighting time itself.
When the world was unaware
of our souls entwined,

the roots of that very tree
hiding beneath
the cracked ground.

On Resistance

ESCAPISM

like the heaviness
of a quiet room   the scent
of your cherry lips
i trace my fingers over
the contours of the day

when

your softness was more
than just a memory

funeral home
a moonlit shadow settles
like second skin

THE WEIGHT OF A PANDEMIC

What is home if not our bodies mingling in sweat, your mouth on my mouth, our bodies sliding and twisting, falling into a river, fishes swimming in a small pond, not missing the ocean, making wild love to pass time.

Your hands on my waist, I forget that we are chained to a bed.

But the fruits are disappearing, the sun is scorching my skin, and the house is a mess. The sheets are stained, my hands are now wrapped against my knees. I am a slow sigh away from falling apart. I don't have to see you go to miss you. I am terrified of the temple sounds of your breathing. Has this love become a prayer? Or, is it a war siren; a warning to duck? My flesh has your flesh to turn to.

rotting apple
a farmer carrying a bag
on hunched shoulders

CHAI, BISCUIT AUR HUM

i.

It's been years
since I've worn that dress.
It hangs upside down in my cupboard.
Even if I throw it away
rip holes in its mid-seam.
Burn it.
It has a way of crawling back to my room
every night.

ii.

He slid his hand up my thigh
and told me I am a moon-flower.
I'd bloom,
every night,
in his arms.

I crossed my legs,
grabbed his hand, balled mine into a fist.
Offered him a cup of tea
and smiled.

My mother appeared behind me.
Did she wonder why my hands trembled?
She left to get biscuits.

I wish she'd known
biscuits weren't all.
He wanted me for breakfast,
or for dinner
whenever she wasn't looking.
Even if he wasn't hungry.
He told me,
"The way to a man's heart
is through his stomach."
He ate me.
Inside out,
and outside in.
With the moon blooming,
my petals bled.

iii.

I met his daughter
when she was as old as me.
When he first tapped my chest
with his fist, a loud knock
on an empty door...
Thoroughly examining me
for signs of growth,
he wanted his teeth to be
my body's welcome mat.
Atithi Devo Bhava,
he whispers.
The Guest is God.

His little girl was
hiding under our bed,
hoping no visitor knocked on her door.
"Don't worry," I tell her.
Atithi Devo Bhava
"I'm entertaining the guest tonight!"

iv.

I see him once every week.
I serve him milky chai.
My mother gets him biscuits
and I smile.

LAST CHRISTMAS

what is home
without your elbows
on my palms
without your tongue
in my mouth
without your lips
pressed against my ears
our bodies twisting and turning
to each other's whims
lovers with their toes pressed
down towards the floorboard
bodies creaking
glistened with sweat
mouths escaping
towards the light
softly glowing
hips moving
in small, concentric circles
to larger, wilder circles
our bodies, a hula-hoop
that starts with one waist
that finishes by embracing the other

what is this home
that reeks of your absence
like a dying man's room
where he said his last words
to a ceiling fan
that kept spinning
round and round
and around
like a full stop hung on a cross
with blue ribbons
they always mean to visit
until they don't
and all these words they
meant to say but didn't
collect on their tongues
like pellets, weighing
down their mouths

we let too much go
too easily, we haven't
learned yet to keep fighting
like our grandmothers used to
be it for love
be it for the chance
to be someone they'd want
to spend a lifetime around

it's never easy for little girls
to love themselves or the
older woman to leave that man
who hasn't hugged her once
in 13 years, and only thinks of her
if there are no eggs on his plate
that morning
she felt chained
to her bed, her limbs had melted

away to the floorboards, just like
the toes of the two lovers she used
to once know, who would look at her
and remember what her mouth tasted like
after they'd had a lot of eggnog
this Christmas, she refused to wake up
and make his eggs, he didn't understand
why she just lay there with her eyes wide open
staring at the creaking fan

Memories We Tied Like Ribbons on Our Necks

There's so much I want to say
to you.

How is mother's knee?
Is she still bruised from when she flew

towards the white wall, her body slowly
sliding down like the bee we squashed

in the summer house you took me to
and I sipped lemonade and kissed your

wine mouth? We used to dream so much
sometimes, the wind took notice

and touched my waist like scattering fireflies.
Sometimes, the squall tasted pain

and huddled close in the pits of my stomach
only your mother understood

with her half smile, the other side of her
mouth still scorched from the heat

of the chai you splashed on her face
like you were an experimental painter

and you could colour us all red
and you did.

After I left you
my eyes only opened

to the inky stain of the sky
my lights leaked out of the

cracked half of my spine.
My back still tingles

when I think of you.
I can't look into a mirror

because my face still has
your fingers mapped out on it.

There are places I visit
and your memory jumps

at me
I'm getting mugged

in a dark alley but I've already given you
everything I had, which is to say,

I don't know how to love myself anymore
because I collected all my love into stars

and put it in your fists.
I want to say please don't release

them just yet, I don't have my light back
but you shake your fists at me

and there goes my light.

What is it about firsts
that you let your knees
kiss the dust of the street?

HUNGER GAMES

Those were really the days
Where we walked wearing masks
And were hit for buying medicines
By cops with large sticks
The vegetable vendor gave me
Broken eggs because he fell to
The ground on his way to my street
The system allows only the rich to
Have sunny side up eggs, the rest
Are on the run

The rice is used for sanitisers
Instead of being boiled with dal
So a mother holds her children and jumps.
Drowning beats starvation on the pain scale.
For, how long could they believe the lie
That this is an adventure? Hunger Games
The richest survive
There is so much food, just not for them
Until they break into a volunteer warehouse
And fight. "Everybody has a story and a history,"[*]
But the hungry are wearing a de-visibility cloak
They are lined up naked outside

The grocery store, and you don't have to see them
Because it's inconvenient and your hands
Are carrying so many bags already

I am baking an upside-down pineapple cake
For my Instagram followers, my screams
Have a taste of their own, my lover licks
My lips and says I am vanilla essence

But the running eggs have made it moist
And my honey so sweet
I wonder how long my hands can bake
Without shaking

Hunger, Roxanne Gay

Trigger Warning

it comes for you when you're not ready
you are never ready
you're watching a movie with your friends
and the woman on screen has her blouse
ripped off by a man but you're the one
grabbing your chest and breathing faster
than the heroine, getting up to run to the
bathroom and fall to the sink
teaching
yourself to inhale and exhale five times
like a *Mimosa* folding in

you walk back into the theatre
no one can see a glistening face in the dark
and no one can
find out what *he* did to you
the salt of the popcorn you've ordered
the crunch against your teeth
focus, focus and munch
forget last year, the same sunset
watched you biting your tongue
to silence a scream.
this is not the first time
a panic attack has wrapped its hands

around your neck to choke
you in public
he used to do it too,
and then he took a scissor and
snipped your lady parts like a
garden weed and your hands
are suddenly on fire.
you, a woman who bleeds
in love yet bereft
starved of love for yourself

you are with your new lover for
one minute
but your kiss is the ex frenching you
without consent
I want to say I am strong,
I make art of the trauma that refuses
to leave my body or memory
but *he* keeps stabbing,
as I am running in a field of blue
orchards, the sky has dropped
on my chest, this freedom is a trap

my sheets bury the filth of my skin,
sometimes for weeks, I remain frozen
time asked if it could sit
beside me and wait with me
the war is over but my body
is waiting for its sirens to loudly
ring in my ears
but the music stopped moving my feet
my spine, a curving bowl of temple sounds
taka takita tha
I have spun for hours
years
in wait

I tell my lover, I will kiss him
another night, and I smile
tonight, we will try sleeping
with the lights turned on

IT IS ALL A NUMBERS GAME

In a country of 1,387,297,452 people
42,800 affected with a virus
that has killed 1,389 Indians.

41st day of lockdown all over India.
269 days of lockdown in Kashmir
without internet. I am tweeting about how

the PM's international trip is costing
22 crores per country.
2021 crores spent so far
on international diplomacy
as the country burns

like the migrant's home.
40 million migrants in Covid-19 lockdown.
200 people killed by hunger.

Mothers drowning with their children
in rivers or at the hands of abusive husbands.
315 cases of Domestic Violence
reported in April alone.
And the ones that went unreported?

3 million sex workers affected.
The government budget and society
have screwed them of their money.

In this game of snakes and ladders
the privileged are slithering up
with forked tongues.

JNU fees hike makes it 60,000 a year.
25 students brutally attacked
protesting for the right to education.
0 arrests made so far.
Their wings clipped by the Right.

200 injured in the Delhi Pogrom.
51 people killed, 35 Muslims.
Since when do the dead have faith?
Or are the religious being killed?

Thousands of women sitting in protests
at Shaheen Bagh, now cleared off because
of the Pandemic.
The clampdown in guise of a lockdown.

It is all a numbers game.
Your bank account decides
whether you're the snake
or the rat in its belly.

POLITICS

1. There has been no food in the house for two days now. The child is wailing, she wants her mother's milk but her mother's breasts are empty; her face crayoned with purple bruises.

2. Hindus refuse to collect food from Muslim volunteers; their hunger swelling up their rage.

3. My people got shredded like string cheese. Politics is the grater.

4. A grandma holds the Buddhist flag and prayer beads and chants Om Mani Padme Hum.

5. The farmer eats plain rice for two months; his vegetables have started to rot.

6. A sex worker walks up to a police officer on the street unafraid of a pandemic. It will kill her slower than starvation.

7. Radha tapes a newspaper over her used sanitary napkin and wears it again. It's either that or her child's pending uniform fees.

8. The Prime Minister comes on TV wearing a mask and only speaks in chaste Hindi. Tamilians like me are frantically searching for a dictionary.

9. Tap your chest thrice and say, 'All is Well', or better still, 'Acche Din Aayenge.'

10. I am writing a poem in a used book because there are no fresh pages for my words. It's history repeating itself as I watch the world crack like a betel nut.

A BEAST LOVES ANOTHER BEAST

I dance all day with temple sounds.
One day, I am Ravana– another day
his wife watching him abduct some woman.

Some days I am a golden deer.

Some days I am the demon itself,
the beast who falls in love with a beast.

How did you begin to move into my body?
I only plucked my heart out of my chest
like a temple offering and asked you
if you'd like a bite.

And you did.

Swallowing every inch
of my skin,
snapping
my spine in half–
a KitKat bar. One half for you,
one half for me.

I have withered so much.
I never let you in,
but how would you stop someone
who breaks doors? You build
iron castle gates in return.
Imprisoning both of us,
in the warp and weft of unbroken doors.

I wanted you in.
I needed you out.

An addiction like cigarettes
I couldn't do without.

You are collapsing my lungs
but I love how you feel
inside my mouth.

ABANDONED POEM

Take this poem
And abandon it
Wreck it midway
Mid-sentence add
A full-stop. distort
The subject with an
Object, replace you
With a suitcase, one
That stays to be left
Leaves to come back
To me, I want to fold
You like a napkin
And wipe my mouth
With you, I want to hold
You with my thighs and
Pull you inside me, just
A mid-day distraction,
A stolen kiss for something
That can never be mine
Except in this
Little abandoned poem

MY GRANDMOTHER DANCES WITH MY LOVER

My boyfriend dances like a goose on Christmas and I'm sitting under a tree of festivities with the cats on my lap. I don't know why we wait for Santa without being believers of the faith or men, with beards or without. I am thinking of my blessings–of granny's hands feeding me halwa–her toothless smile–soft and supple skin. I want to bite her cheeks like an apple. We loved Shahid Kapoor before he became a masochist. Mother yells and reminds me, *think of blessings kanna not boys*. So, I think of babies and how lucky I am to not be a mother like her. Mother has the laugh that can split the ground like an earthquake–a gentle rumble. She bakes a chocolate cake and my hands are brown–my mouth, sweet and gooey.

Grandmother–swimming with me in a maxi and suddenly I wish my bikini could float around me like an upside down umbrella. Granny carries our weight so easily–just like that. We are watching the moon from the pool and it feels like the stars wink, and just for a moment there...

Grandma and I went somewhere she'd never been.

WHEN MY MOTHER WAS NOT MY MOTHER

when my mother was not my mother
I was not her daughter which is to say in an
alternate dimension a small probability
existed where *I didn't*
my mother didn't
have to carry me on her shoulders always like this
that her knees unbuckled at her
own will and not by the weight of my
mistakes

mother was so much before she became a mother, *my*
mother was wild-carefree, a little cracked, a little healed -
mother was another woman, her lithe hands buried in the
pages of a book instead of wrist-deep in a sodden sink
doing dishes under our kitchen faucet, mother knew how
to ask for the world she wanted without pretending it was
just us

mother sighed and touched herself at night–her body
smouldering under faint moonlight–mother bought herself
a blouse the colour of sunflowers, in the absence of

sunlight, the flowers turn to each other for comfort–*that's family*, mother says letting her hair drop to the ache of her waist–shimmering black–even the descending of a nightfall of stars couldn't dim her light. her smile knocks on our door only sometimes now. on days full of traditions.

does mother wonder what
life she would lead if she
didn't labour over me? I
want to tell her, mother,
sometimes I wonder for
you too.

SADNESS

It's easier to tell yourself
Sadness is coming
Because your lover left

Give me a stranger to shame,
I am too scared to look within
And discover I am broken

Mother, I am trying so hard
To stay alive despite all this
Darkness wrapping itself

Around my body,
Wipe your tears father
I am still in the fight

The depressed are not ungrateful
Just full of shame
The boulder of sadness

Weighs me down

My mouth refuses to let
My words spill, my tongue
Is holding on to my poems
For support

I feel so alone,
When the lights are out
You can't see them smiling
At you

Forgive me mother,

I feel lost,

All my roads start and end

At the edge of my bed,

My feet

Buried in white sheets

That will soon turn turmeric,

I will smell like a rotting corpse

Without having died.

My lighthouse,
My body, my sea,
The storm, the cold
And the rotting fish
Where do I go from here?

My poem will never find you
But I'll keep trying mother

To keep fighting
Till my words rest in peace
At your feet

Sadness comes knocking
And the lover leaves
I hold sadness
The way I once held you
You fled with my colour

water lilies
need to bloom
in a cold dark room

ADVICE

Don't shake hands
when the State has washed
its hands of us.
Pandemic kills.

HOME

I am walking into a home I invented
I was lonely and you were nowhere to be seen
I don't miss you if I create you
The only war of ours is separation
Our bodies do not erase this touch,
What I call a memory,
What you call an inconvenience
You remain inconsistent,
I am inconsolable

I thought I could seal you with a kiss
A stamp, but you pushed me out
And kept my mouth
How many hungry poems
Have you buried behind my bruised gums?

I want it all back,
All of you
I want you to lose yourself to mist
Standing in front of me
You, a steam-kettle, you whistle
And suddenly,
I'm mist,
A mis-fit
Semi-state
In longing

DOWN

It's true, when you're in love, it's a feeling
in the stomach, like fireflies, or a knife wound,
synonyms
for the kind of love you give me
I grew up wanting fireworks in a man,
Is that why my men explode?
I want to catch your heat and flick the match right back at you
I want to hurt you with these words, the way you hurt me withou
This is just another poem you don't like reading, so maybe I'll
read it to you as I bend down on my knees and watch you sleep
to never wake up,
I want to love
you and bite your tongue off so for once the room can warm itse
with my words. I stepped on a piece of land
that forgot its summer sun,
I am cold and naked, there is a frost
where a warm heart once beat itself
in love for me, there is no distance as invisible as a lover dining
with his once-loved, there is no more longing for what they lost, as
much as losing what they once longed for, I want you to notice m
just once, so I can remind myself that I really exist, sometimes, I t
To forget I have a life so it hurts less that
I want to take it away as much

Maybe if you finally read this one poem,
you'll know I am a candle burning;
that every day of loving you, I drop a centimetre in height.
Trip me, I loved with my eyes open,
but my eyelids are glued to my
eyebrows, my pupils popped wide, my jaw agape
I write poems
As dark as my skin, your friends tell me all that
you did when I wasn't
Looking, all that you told me happened like
the future telling history
what will happen next, I died when we met,
and I may be birthed
when I finally leave.

This poem is a lie.
You are not toxic.
I love you.
I need you.

FOR MY FATHER'S BIRTHDAY

I give him his greatest present
and hide my death wish
to greet him instead.

I try to be a good daughter
I taught him to expect less
each day, like every ungood daughter
does. he went from *top your class*
to *stay*. alive. it only took 5 attempts to
kill myself for him to understand
this pain I feel of living

the first time, I was 13, I ran
away from home with his t-shirt
wrapping a knife I hid in my bag
and I walked outside Nerul station
and sat on the footpath at 11 pm

the knife slicing my thin wrists
when I started bleeding
I started walking back home, wondering
if the blood trail would last all the way back

papa came running, and swept me
in his arms, breathless, his tears
damp on my shoulder sleeve

the second time was easier,
I swallowed 70 pills

and they pumped it out me
so I got a septum piercing
for my nose to obliterate the pipes
and feel beautiful again, like I wanted to
on the inside.

the third time, I fell in love
and I thought a boy who owned my body
deserved my life, and father stood silently
and asked me if my family didn't love me enough

for me to want to try to feel a little

more alive but love was never enough. the
wars never stopped

how do I begin
to tell a father that his daughter was pulled
inside out between her thighs?

some conversations are only meant for the
listening so the fourth time, father never found

out but I drank Dettol in a school trip and then tried to
jump off a roof,
only by the fifth time, did I
realise I was as bad at killing myself as I was
at living, so that's another thing I can't seem to do
just right.

father knows I now live with a boy
who has a beautiful smile and kind eyes.
the boy says I'm beautiful but he never
touches me like I really am

he is walking on eggshells, afraid
I will break like a noodlestring, I want to tell
him I have learnt to lie. just like he does.

I tell myself I am beautiful. I am strong.
I will survive.

SHOT BY A SHOOTING STAR

emptying my body
into your opened palms
I am a soft woman with a loud heart
make a fist and tap my waist
I need to stop pouring out
and save myself tonight

tonight, a shooting star
cracked my window glass
and I gladly wished it was coming
for my heart, cupid has it caged
my Dvorak dreams of violins

violins made us hope our skies
sighed as one tonight, even for only a moment
we lay there, sighing hopelessly in love
without ever having really said it to each other
Did this sudden spring give us
hope or meaning–I want to tell you how I feel
but I'm scared of polluting our air
with language–this air thick with burden
my heaviness rests on your lips

my heart
a little string I throw towards you

you
catch me,
I want to say
I've spiralled alone
my moon is tired of

this eclipse, share
my loud heart–hold me
tender, undress me slowly
I want to hear you say
soft woman, stay

stay, with your loud heart
longing for mine

City Lights and its Underbelly

I

How do I tell you Amma,
that I skipped dinner last night
because a delivery man
who tried to break through my door
spilt all the Tom Yum soup on my floor
but the cats lapped it up
and rolled around in it
like snow angels in Novosibirsk's cold
and as I shoved him out of my home
I wondered where I hung the mistletoe.

I called you as I sat on the floor cross-legged,
heard you talk about the ghastly rape of a three-year-old
child
in Gurgaon who was bludgeoned to death
by a 20-year-old man and I wondered
if you'd feel as disgusted if I told you
what happened to your own three-year-old.
you see, mother we
live in houses with glass windows

we're always worried about those lurking in our
backyards
but mother, we have been sleep-walking our way
ghosts in our own beds
which is to say I don't know how to make
my tongue speak again
but maybe, somehow
there must be something magical about our bloodline
because I, my lost voice
silenced everyone who ever found out.

II

I'm 22 and I carry a Swiss knife in my pocket
And I tell you ma, that cities leave a certain taste in my
mouth
like Bombay was salty seaweed dipped
in Patti's white *thayir vadais*
but Gurgaon tastes like rusting iron and dead blood
in my mouth
because I'm tired of biting off
the flesh of men who come at me.
they drive around in top-end cars
with their caste displayed on the trunks
men roaming around with hockey sticks on their
shoulders
To think this is why my grandmother
ceremoniously prepared me in 1999,
scrubbing my face with *haldi* and *besan*
to remedy my dark-skin
because I needed to be fair and lovely
because the magazines that my classmates held
tell people that being fair-skinned is
the only way they'd ever be seen
I was invisible and I knew this
because Mother, I spent so much time

hiding in school bathrooms, finishing
Oliver Twist and Dickens' tome about loneliness
to the sound of the flush and the haze of stale urine.

Amma, there's so much I want to say to you,
instead, I tell you how sorry
I feel for the three-year-old's torn family
I tell you how much I love you
but I still have hope,
that women will go on to be safe spaces for each other
but we have so much fire,
we burnt your farmlands 20 years ago
and all you seem to be doing in Gurgaon
is whitening your faces
from the shame that darkened it.

THEY LIE AND TELL US
After Preeti Vangani

They lie and tell us
they respect us and they care
that we are more than bodies
to hold and grunt with, they tell us
to talk loudly, scream our truths from rooftops
that we have been vilified but have not been defeated.
they tell us to post stories on
Instagram, rants on Facebook and feminist
punchlines on Twitter. they tell us
that they want us to have jobs because
our golden beauty buttocks are attached
to a brain and because beauty fades but
our work stays. they tell us they understand
consent and they don't condone harassment
and women are Goddesses. they tell us
they want us to study and be the centre of
battlelines because it is time
for women to shine. they tell us they support us.
they tell us we have a voice. to use our voice.
to use our stage. our stand. our sit-in protests. our poems.
they tell me this poem can become a manifesto of their
allegiance.

until they reach the second half of this poem
and realise that they are really the woke boys
with a mouth full of sinfree words and
hands of blood. that they choke our voice with one
elbow
and beckon us to speak with the other.
that the schools are on streets
where our girls get beaten for walking in daylight.
That they hoist us on a
pedestal in temples
and grab our ankles in the courtyard.
you call us jaana, aye chokri, randi, saali, kuttiya, moti
bhains, sexy, pataka. we call you abusers. sometimes,
you call us a friend and invite us in for tea. we follow
because a woman's heart is a phoenix. we follow
because we trust in a revolution that calls for
redemption.

BLOOM

This is a poem bursting with hope. In this poem, the oceans are not drying, and the chinar leaves are not rooted in the bloody waters of the Jhelum. The sky is not enveloped with the sour whisk of pollution and the birds are singing aloud in clean air. The sky is dressed like a bride, decked in a blood-red saree that unveils into a brilliant peacock blue. My father named me after clouds that caressed our mud-brown roof top. The clouds would loom over our heads swelling with promise. In this poem, it only rains for the plants to nod their heads. Shake some buds and our laps will be decked with fallen wildflowers. The Earth came to me in a dream and wept. I woke up in the middle of the dream and fell right into this poem. I feel so glad to be alive, this moment. Brimming with the gossamer magnitude of hope; the possibility of life. Mid-bloom.

Our people are not drowning and the water doesn't fill the streets. The ground doesn't quake and break our homes. The dogs have a comfy roof and the cats are happily lazing under the shade of a tree. Slaughterhouses burst into orchid farms and even the chickens are grazing with the sheep. My humans are unslimy. No, they haven't grown snake skin. The animals still haven't found a cage large enough to imprison them. The ice caps stay frozen and the pandas aren't abandoned on a broken iceberg. I can open my windows and let my cats leave with my sadness, and know for certain that only my cats will return. Bloom.

The scent looms in the air. You can inhale nature's seductive perfume and your lungs would walk out of nicotine's life. The 13-year-olds will go to school and will not have to sit outside of government offices protesting to save the Mother that birthed us.

Look. This poem slides off a rainbow and falls on us like dew drops. I felt afraid to sleep tonight because our Mother will return. I'm afraid to fall asleep because of the beauty this world holds in every wink, that is all I want to gather. But we take so much more than we leave behind and Earth can only shrug. Broken fragments, mid-bloom.

I want to carry our mother's cracked soles on my bare shoulders. Burning in angst, her wild-heart fire is now burning this poem, my palms, my tongue, my hope-filled chest. I finally slept at night and dreamed I was walking in an open field of jasmines. In bloom, the sun shone on my back. The clouds staggered to my feet and asked if I wanted to bury my footprints. The Earth was no longer weeping. Where do I bury you mother? Mid-bloom, I stopped existing in the hope that this poem gives you life. Bloom freely.

ACKNOWLEDGEMENTS

This book started many years ago when I first discovered poetry. Kartik, my best friend, who first nurtured my love for poetry, thank you. Sonal, Nandini, Manjiri, Srishti, Aparajita, Ram, and Zahra, thank you for always believing in my work on days that I couldn't. Paresh Tiwari and Vinita Ramchandani for editing my book and supporting me every step of the way. Amma, Appa, and Paati for being such a significant presence in all of my poems and accepting me unconditionally for the rebel I am. I'll always be grateful to Nikhil, my partner, through this terrifying and exhilarating journey. This book is for you, my love. Thank you to everyone who made this dream happen. Here is the moment that makes me want to keep fighting and keep surviving.

MEGHNA PRAKASH

Meghna is the founder of *Poetry Dialogue*, a platform that promotes daily poetry for the accessibility of poems and publishing opportunities. Meghna's poetry has been published in several journals, including the *Ethos Literary Journal*, *The Bengaluru Review*, *The Alipore Post*, *Ruptured Anthology*, *Scroll*, *Kritya Magazine*, among others. She has performed in India, Russia, Nepal, Sri Lanka, Boston, and Bhutan. She has done performances for *The American Centre*, *Kommune*, *Airplane Poetry Movement*, *Unerase Poetry*, and at *mental health and poetry festivals* in India. Meghna is mental health, trauma, and peace activist.